AFTER 50

Reviews of Previous Spirituality Books by Robert J. Wicks

A Circle of Friends (1996)
(with Robert Hamma)

"...a lovely book. Like friendship itself, the chapters delight, console, and challenge us."

> —Evelyn Eaton Whitehead
> and James D. Whitehead
> Authors, *Shadows of the Heart*

Seeds of Sensitivity (1995)

"*Seeds of Sensitivity* should be read by everyone, especially those who live their lives in service to others."

> —Joseph Cardinal Bernardin
> Archbishop of Chicago

Touching the Holy (1992)

"The lucid direction for ordinary everyday prayer that this book offers is particularly helpful in a time which often prizes the extraordinary."

> —Constance FitzGerald, O.C.D.
> Author, "Impasse and the
> Dark Night of the Soul"

Seeking Perspective (1991)

"A beautiful vision of the action of grace and the movementS of the human heart."   —Robert F. Morneau

> Author, **Mantras for the Morning**

Availability (1986)

"*Availability* is sharp in insight, powerful in its simplicity...It is a truly healing and refreshing experience to read this book and savor it page by page."

> —Bernard J. Tyrrell, S.J.
> Author, *Christotherapy*

AFTER 50

~ Spiritually Embracing Your Own *Wisdom Years* ~

Robert J. Wicks

~ A Gift of Pure Hope from the Author of the Bestseller *Touching the Holy* ~

Paulist Press
New York / Mahwah, N.J.

Cover design by Lynn Else

Book design by Kathleen Doyle

Library of Congress Cataloging-in-Publication Data

Wicks, Robert J.
    After 50 : spiritually embracing your own wisdom years / Robert J. Wicks.
        p. cm.
    Includes bibliographical references.
    ISBN 978-0-8091-4674-1
    1. Middle aged persons—Religious life. 2. Spiritual life—Christianity. I. Title.
    BV4579.5.W53 1997
    248.8'4—dc21

                                                                96-45267
                                                                     CIP

Published by Paulist Press
997 Macarthur Boulevard
Mahwah, New Jersey 07430

www.paulistpress.com

Printed and bound in the
United States of America

CONTENTS

Introduction... 1

I. Praying... 7

II. Caring... 35

III. Nurturing... 57

Epilogue... 79

Notes... 83

Readings... 86

Dedication

For My Wife Michaele...
Through All the Years, a True
Anamcara

Introduction

People are anxious to save up financial means for old age; they should also be anxious to prepare a spiritual means for old age... Wisdom, maturity, tranquility do not come all of a sudden when we retire..."
—Abraham Joshua Heschel[1]

Several months ago I was walking with a spiritual mentor through the Virginia countryside on a sunny crisp winter day. About half-way through our usual route along the Shenandoah River, he surprised me with the comment: "I think now may be a good time for you to take your spiritual life more seriously."

Although the statement seemed quite accurate to me at the time, later I wondered why I had not reacted more defensively to it. After all, for almost two years I had been driving one and one-half hours each way, every six weeks or so, to see him. I really felt I had been investing good time and energy in being more open to the deeper elements in my life. So, my natural response could well have been: "Well, what do you think I have been doing?"

However, I think the ideal timing and accuracy of his comment, as well as the trust I had in him and our relationship, made me see his words much differently. What I instantly felt he was trying to tell me was that it was time to leap more freely and deeply into what was truly important in life. It was time to *really:*

—Seek and embrace God at the center of my life;

—Care for others from a deeper place in my soul; and

—Nurture my own interior life through creative, new, and simple ways.

To do this, for my part, my attitude had to change profoundly so what was truly important would be at the center of my life. I also needed at this crucial stage of my life—I was just turning 50 years of age—to understand more fully what it meant to live in a noble way and to possess one of the greatest fruits of deep trust in God: namely, *a hopeful heart.* In this way, not only would I be able to live this stage of my life more gently and faithfully but also I might be able to help others even better than I had in the past.

My whole professional life has been devoted in some way to the nurturing of a hopeful heart—mine and those with whom I have journeyed as a therapist, author, supervisor, colleague, mentor, educator, family member, and friend. Now, after hearing the above statement from my own mentor I have come to believe that such a nurturing process is very important to help instill perspective, passion, and commitment to what is noble in life *now.* In addition, it is also essential to help us prepare for the *"spiritual wisdom years"*—a time when we are called to embrace and share our spiritual knowledge and experiences in a freer and more generous way with others.

Upon reflection on all of this, I recognized as well that when asked by people to break down my philosophy and spirituality, three words repeatedly came to mind.

They are *praying, caring,* and *nurturing.* By this I mean: praying to God; caring for others; and nurturing self.

And so, with these three simple words in mind (and the belief that other persons might find my comments and approach of some help) I have prepared this little book on nurturing the interior life. My hope is that in walking together through the thoughts, feelings, stories and prayers on the following pages, both the reader and I will be better able to structure a way of spiritually embracing this gentle and holy time in our lives.

These steps are *not* taken just for our own benefit. Rather, they are taken so that while we are meeting our destiny, others who come into contact with us can embrace their God-given destiny as well. One of the most essential quests for people after they turn fifty years of age is not only to embrace the empowerment of God themselves (important as this is), but also to simultaneously model it for others.

For as Nelson Mandela said forcefully in his 1994 Inaugural Speech:

> Our deepest fear is not that we are inadequate. Our deepest fear is that we are powerful beyond measure. It is our light, not our darkness, that most frightens us. We ask ourselves who are we to be brilliant, gorgeous, talented, fabulous? Actually, who are we not to be? We are a child of God. Our playing small doesn't serve the world...We were born to make manifest the glory of God that is within us; it is in *Everyone!* And as we let our own light shine, we unconsciously give other people permission to do the same. As we are liberated from

our own fear, *our presence automatically liberates others!* (Emphasis added.)

After 50 is, in essence, then, meant to provide a clear and loud "Amen" to this call for shared and enhanced liberation during the time we refer to as...*Our Wisdom Years!*

—*Robert J. Wicks*

I

Praying

Prayer requires education, training, reflection, contemplation. It is not enough to join others; it is necessary to build a sanctuary within, brick by brick.
—Abraham Joshua Heschel[2]

The interior life, where our prayer experiences thrive, is a place of truth and love. It is a setting in which we hope to meet God. It is also a place to set aside created whims so they don't crowd out our genuine deeply felt spiritual needs. Such essential needs include:

> a need for permanence in a civilization of transience;
>
> a need for the Absolute when all else is becoming relative;
>
> a need for silence in the midst of noise;
>
> a need for gratuitousness in the face of unbelievable greed;
>
> a need for poverty amid the flaunting of wealth;
>
> a need for contemplation in a century of action, for without contemplation, action risks becoming mere agitation;

a need for communication in a universe content with entertainment and sensationalism;

a need for peace amid today's universal outbursts of violence;

a need for quality to counterbalance the increasingly prevalent response to quantity;

a need for humility to counteract the arrogance of power and science;

a need for human warmth when everything is being rationalized or computerized;

a need to belong to a small group rather than to be part of the crowd;

a need for slowness to compensate the present eagerness for speed;

a need for truth when the real meaning of words is distorted in political speeches and sometimes even in religious discourses;

a need for transparency when everything seems opaque.

Yes, a need for *the interior life...*[3]

The interior life, though, is something for which we need to educate and prepare ourselves. As in the case of financial retirement, the earlier we begin to prepare the better. Also, no matter what our age, there are still steps we can take now to enrich our inner life and the lives of those we meet.

This is especially important for us to realize so we can:

—Educate our young people to nurture and sustain their inner life;

—Remind those in their twenties, thirties, and forties not to lose sight of "the spiritual" at the expense of seemingly more pressing practical needs; and

—Encourage persons in their fifties and older to:

Reap what they have sowed spiritually;

Deepen their current lives of faith; and

Share freely with others what they have learned through their past experiences of God.

And, probably the best beginning for this realization, is to seek a better understanding of the key elements of the interior life as well as to examine several basic helpful approaches to prayer.

The Interior Life[4]

Our "interior," "inner," or "spiritual" life must take into account the needs and tendencies of the whole person. In addition, each of us as individuals is unique and therefore must respond in accord with his or her own uniqueness. Yet, even though this be the case, in the broad sense, there are several attitudes/behaviors as well as individual and communal actions that are capable of nurturing the "spiritual" dimension of life.

The first is (to borrow a phrase from Brother Lawrence[5]) the "practice of the presence of God." Because many of us have been raised on strong doses of dualism, this is not as easy as it sounds. Attending to God's presence in prayer, worship, "holy" reading, good company, joy-filled events, and good fortune takes (at least initially) conscious awareness and effort. However, ferreting out God's presence at the opposite end of the continuum takes something more.

In the face of suffering, illness, pain, failure, discouragement (whether one's own or someone else's) it is essential not only to make the effort to be consciously God-connected but also to do so with great patience, tenacity, and faith in Julian of Norwich's understanding that "all shall be well." You may not be pleased with the outcome, but nevertheless "all shall indeed be well."

Patience and perseverance are habits that can sustain our faith in times of trial but they do not appear magically and in full bloom when crises present themselves. Rather, they develop (or flounder) over time in accord with how we deal with life's little inconveniences, and this requires *discipline*—a forgotten value in these times, unfortunately.

This brings us to a second point, which is the relationship between discipline and freedom. The interior life requires ample doses of both to remain in balance.

Some of us require greater discipline/structure than others, but all of us need at least some discipline for healthy living. The goal is not to get locked into a routine that is so heavily structured and rigidly disciplined that we miss encountering the holy because at 8:45 a.m. *every* morning, no matter what or who tries to interfere, we go to our room to pray. On the other hand, the often glib comment, "my life is a prayer," is too often far from the truth. If we are to have a rich interior life it is essential to prioritize our God relationship by setting aside special times, places, and occasions for prayer. Like our human relationships, our God relationship needs time, attention, effort, and *love* if it is to develop and grow.

Love is the concept underlying the third point and also pointing back to point two. Love dictates the balance between structure and freedom, thus allowing us the possibility of meeting God in the mundane as well as in the "sacred." By the same token it moves us to seek a balance between action and contemplation. By nature each of us is drawn more toward one direction than the other, and it is not always easy to balance the scales.

It is better to imagine action-contemplation interacting in a circular mode rather than as a scale or a continuum. The circular image allows us to see more readily the necessity for each to flow into the other. Each in turn is a source and resource for the other.

As Teresa of Avila says, we are not "bodiless souls." Therefore, the prayer of our hearts must blossom into love for those outside ourselves in very tangible ways. At the same time, the joys and sorrows of the world outside (both near and far) must seep into our hearts and color our relationship with God. So, in essence, on a practical level, we need to develop a *contemplative attitude toward life in general* if we are to nurture and sustain a rich healthy inner life.

Several ways we can do this are by:

1. *Listening* (a very important word) to the people and the world around us, because it is in and through people and events that we encounter God and what God is calling us to be;

2. *Prioritizing* the God-relationship in our lives by recognizing the importance of both personal and communal prayer and then acting accordingly;

3. *Reading and praying with scripture* where we encounter God's self-revelation most directly;

4. *Maintaining a healthy balance* between structure and freedom; action and contemplation; personal and communal prayer/worship;

5. Making efforts to nurture our faith through *spiritual reading, good conversation, and on-going education;*

6. *Opening ourselves* (despite the pain that may be associated with it) to the possibilities of grace that fill and surround us and sometimes the kinds of grace that even come kicking, scratching, or begging at our door.

And so, the interior life then is not an imaginary or psychotic world. It is not a place to run to so we can pout, brood, fantasize revenge, or to ruminate over things as a way to mentally beat ourselves up. Instead, as we have seen it is a place of self-knowledge, self-nurturance, challenge, and solid peace. It is a place that will not only be our strength but also one that we can offer to others. When our interior life is strong, our attitude toward others is gentle. When our inner life feels nourished, our hearts can be open to others' pain.

In a reflection on our time together, one person whom I journeyed with said: "And what will I leave

behind from our relationship: my 'stuckness,' my uncon-
sciousness, my shame and guilt, my repressed pain,
resentment and depression...And what will I take with
me? What will be awakened through the gift of our relationship? My playfulness, my love of life, my sense of
wonder, my gratitude, my openness, and my wholeness."

Unfortunately, though, our inner life is often
infected by some of the negative "atmosphere" of our
upbringing. For instance, Gorky in his autobiography
said: "Grandfather's house was filled with a choking fog
of mutual hostility. It poisoned the grown-ups and even
infected the children."[6]

Our response to such influences is to build a persona
inside that is filled with fear, hesitancy, prickliness, and
anger—not a very gentle place for us to center ourselves
and greet life or form an attitude to welcome others.

Moreover, when our inner life is narrow and distorted, our understanding, appreciation, and grasp of life
also suffer dramatically. Carl Jung, the famous Swiss psy-
chiatrist, put it in these terms:

> People become neurotic when they content
> themselves with inadequate or wrong answers
> to the question of life. They seek position, mar-
> riage, reputation, outward success or money,
> and remain unhappy and neurotic even when
> they have attained what they were seeking.
> Such people are usually confined within too
> narrow a spiritual horizon...If they are enabled
> to develop more spacious personalities, the
> neurosis generally disappears.

What he is speaking about here is the inner life, the
spiritual life, the one we all long for as a way of finding a
deep well within ourselves which will remain calm and

pure no matter how stormy, violent, or polluted the inter-
personal "weather" around us becomes.

The inner life is important because it impacts every
aspect of our living since we interpret all aspects of life
via this inner sense of self and the world. For instance,
one person who was once sexually abused at a very
young age said at the end of therapy that, early in her life,
transitions seemed abrupt, fearful, and everything
seemed worse after them. "Now that I am in a different
place in my heart," she said, "transitions are to be
reached out to with wonder and awe."

The state of our interior life *does* make a difference
to others. When we have a gentle, healthy, and strong
inner life, we are part of the healing stillness in the world
which offers places of hope to all who suffer and yearn
for justice, solace, and encouragement. But if we, like so
many others, do not feel at home within ourselves, and by
ourselves, we will then add to the sense in the world that
nowhere is there a safe and good place.

This is a very dangerous situation not only for us but
also for the young who follow and try to model themselves after us. Ten years ago one pediatrician noted to
me that she saw the light go out in the eyes of many fifth
and sixth graders—now she sees this same sad shroud
over their spontaneity in the second and third grades.

So, we need to build our inner life piece by piece
today with sensitivity to the need in us for *patience and
perseverance, spiritual sanity,* and *self-knowledge.* Not
just for us do we do this but also for those we meet who
count on us to help them find fresh spiritual water to drink.

Patience and Perseverance

Hopefully, with wisdom comes a recognition of the
value of patience and perseverance. The world is often

rushing to its grave at a time when only immediate gratification seems acceptable and worthwhile, whereas the spiritual life sees timing, faithfulness, hope, and the willingness to act based on what is good and right (rather than just what is merely useful) as essential.

I think the following story, in which the snail symbolizes the spiritual and the sparrows a secular outlook, clearly makes this point:

> A snail ever so slowly walked across the ground toward a cherry tree under the watchful eyes of noisy sparrows in a large oak tree nearby. Then he started ever so slowly again climbing up the tree toward the newly green spring leaves high above.
>
> When the sparrows nearby saw this, they laughed and laughed at him. Finally one flew over and said: "You fool, don't you know there are no cherries up there?"
>
> And, as the snail kept slowly moving up toward the top of the tree he cheerfully replied: "Well, there will be when I get there!"[7]

Patience and perseverance are words that we can put back into the vocabulary of today's secular world if we are spiritually wise. However, we ourselves must know them by heart.

Spiritual Sanity

Recently I was in a bookstore and saw an advertisement posted above a diary purportedly written by Nicole Brown Simpson, a young woman violently murdered along with the male friend who was visiting her. The ad said: "The most eagerly anticipated book of all time is finally here!" I thought wryly to myself: "Well, so much for sacred scripture, Shakespeare and the classics." And the following saying from Abba Anthony, the spiritual father of the fourth century desert movement, came to mind:

> The time is coming when people will be insane
> and when they see someone who is not insane,
> they will attack that person saying: "You are
> insane because you are not like us."

Just as patience and perseverance are building blocks of the inner life, so is the willingness to see life differently. Spiritual sanity requires us to ask of ourselves questions about our life and values. Such questioning allows us to embrace the words of sacred scripture and the tenets of our faith, so when we are called to offer a perspective on life to others who are lost, we do not become enmeshed in a similar secular framework ourselves.

Abraham Heschel, a favorite spiritual guide of mine through his writings, once said: "We teach children how to measure, how to weigh; we fail to teach them how to revere, how to sense wonder and awe. The sense of the sublime, the sign of moral greatness of the human soul and something which is potentially given to [everyone] is now a rare gift."[8]

Why is this so? Maybe it is so because we don't begin preparing our children for their "wisdom years" in the correct way. Maybe we fail to see the path of holiness ourselves and therefore feel inadequate to help them at an early age to seek it. And so, we need to break through the routines of secularism with the meaning of life.

My wife who is a religion teacher for primary grades tells me there is a time-honored tradition in her school, and it is this: Students from kindergarten and the first grade may with their teachers' encouragement go into another class and interrupt the lessons in progress. They do this for a very special purpose which they boldly announce through the use of a sign atop a stick which one of the group holds. The sign says: *"Poetry Break."*

Once they enter the room, they stand in front and wait for silence. After all is quiet they each recite a piece of poetry, thank the class for their attention, and leave. Would that we could have some of these poetry breaks in our businesses, at faculty meetings in universities such as mine, or even in some of our churches to remind all of us of what is truly important and valued in life!

Spiritual sanity requires us to question the voices that are guiding our lives. It asks of us to determine what inner and world values are leading us to believe, think, feel, and act the way we do. If we are to do this, we must have a critical eye for what is around us. Furthermore, we need a keen sense of what we know and believe about ourselves as well—in other words, we must know the simple truths about ourselves. We must have self-knowledge.

Self-Knowledge

Key elements for the spiritual life probably differ from person to person depending upon personality, environment, vocation, etc. However, three essentials are love, detachment, and true humility. And the one underlying prerequisite without which the others would flounder is *self-knowledge.*

When we look at our lives I am sure our experiences will bear out that self-knowledge is the one ongoing element which continues to surprise us with new information. Nothing yet has come along to convince me that self-knowledge can be safely abandoned at any point along "the Way." However, the pursuit does have the inherent danger of allowing unhealthy self-preoccupation to masquerade as self-knowledge. Therefore, it is essential that our self-knowledge be well-laced with honesty, humility, and external validation—which obviously is not easy!

Spiritual leaders as diverse as Muhammad and Teresa of Avila tell us that to truly know ourselves helps us to know God better. However, given our foibles, defenses and past sins, most of us are probably more in accord with Goethe's view of self-knowledge: "Know thyself? If I knew myself, I'd run away!" Yet, without true self-knowledge of both our gifts and growing edges, our progress in the spiritual life will be, at best, erratic.

Although love, detachment, true humility and self-knowledge are—and become increasingly—intertwined, real honest self-knowledge underpins the other three traits as follows:

Without self-knowledge we cannot learn to *love freely* and without conditions; we cannot, in other words, move in the direction of loving as God loves us;

Without self-knowledge we are also unable to recognize the idols from which we need to *detach ourselves* in order to meet God. Consequently, in such instances we cannot develop the detachment necessary for the true caring and compassion of unselfish love; and finally,

Both self-knowledge and loving freely and without condition require an openness and a willingness to be vulnerable in a way that can only take hold and grow in an atmosphere of *true humility.*

Having said all of this, what seems evident is that all four elements (love, detachment, true humility, and self-knowledge) could respond well to the call of the inner life to be ordinary and (in simple ways) be open and responsive to the Spirit. And the underlying movement to do this in our lives is captured by the one central activity of the spiritual life: *prayer.*

Prayer

Sharing ideas and hopes about prayer is a little like giving directions on how to find "the tubes" in London based on experiences of riding on a subway in the United States. We can give a little bit of direction (both the tubes and subways run underground); we can tell about some of their advantages, and probably give a few hints regarding some of the cautions and possible dangers involved in riding them...but that's about it.

Prayer is unique. One of the best ways for each person to pray is to...well, pray! When we take out time alone in silence and solitude, we may feel awkward, but feeling that way is an honest beginning. In communal prayer, we may feel it's all a bit staged, but at least we're together and have the right spirit. The main suggestion then one can give about prayer—whether together or alone—is *do it.* Many of us seem to have a hard time praying. We don't seem to have enough time. Or, even if we do have a quiet free period, our prayers seem to sometimes fall short of what we wish them to be.

Given this, reflecting on how to make some basic starts on developing or deepening our prayer life may be of help. Elsewhere (in *Seeds of Sensitivity,* Ave Maria Press, 1995) I pointed out why people resist meeting God in prayer (and no, it's not that we're too busy). Here I would like instead to offer a few ideas and encouragements on what may help us to develop a vibrant prayer life as well as continue to be faithful to it on a regular basis. The elements I would like to include among some basic ways to pray are:

Conversations with God and formal prayers;

Reflections during the day;

Silence and solitude;

Spiritual letter-writing;

Developing your own parables.

Conversations with God and formal prayers represent one of the best known cornerstones of the spiritual life. Many people from the time they were young would take out time during the day or week to "talk with God." Even when this is not done, people will say they do it during a sickness or loss, when they feel deep gratitude for a request granted, or wish to repent for something they have done for which they are experiencing shame.

Two additional suggestions I would make about conversational prayer are that we try to be more *regular* and *honest* in our conversations. We should open a dialogue with God during the normal times (if there are such things!) in our life. Then, when extraordinary events come up, we will not feel such a stranger to God. But for us to do this we must give conversational prayer with God the time it needs so our spiritual relationship can develop. Obviously this is not easy today.

A number of years ago I treated a physician with one of the busiest medical practices around. He was having an extra-marital affair. If I were to see him now I think my first reaction, given his busy clinical work load, would be: "Where does he get the time?"

Time seems to be such a precious commodity now. Yet we must be willing to spend time with God if we expect this central relationship in our life to deepen.

Complete honesty is also important. Real spirituality dawns when God becomes as real as the problems and joys we face each day. There is a natural tendency to edit our conversations with God. When we do this our censored conversations tend to turn into boring, lifeless, meaningless ones.

Conversational prayer should *not* exclude our experiences of anger and joy, our doubts and confusions, and all that happens in our leisure time, family life, finances, work-a-day world, and even our sex-life. (Yes, God knows how all the parts work. I am sure, when we talk with God about our intimate relations, all in the heavens do not stop everything and start saying to each other: "Did you know that it worked that way?" "No, did you?") Our conversational prayer must include *details, emotions* and *real life concerns* if our relationship via this type of communication with God is to blossom.

In line with this, instead of hiding from God, we should also be willing to share when we are presently refusing to change or don't want healing. Honest prayer is always preferable to not discussing something with God. So, if you are drinking too much, are having an affair outside of marriage, are too concerned about your image, refuse to confront an injustice, or are cheating someone, then this should be shared with God. It is better than avoiding these topics; we must share deep feelings even when we feel we are letting God down.

For instance, if you hate someone, you can tell God this: "I know I am being petty and trying to undercut this person and it is wrong. But I refuse to change my behavior now. If you want to work a miracle to change me or have the *Parousia* (Second Coming of the Lord) now, that's fine. You're God. But I am not forgiving this individual. I even think you have made a mistake in creating him. It is just like the time you made ostriches—those silly animals are a mistake of creation and so is he."

Whether it is a problematic relationship, a bad habit or an addiction, whatever...the important goal for us is to share our inability to let go of something with God instead of hiding it. Hiding things from God goes hand in hand with hiding things from ourselves. Recognizing problems even in prayer, maybe especially in prayer, is a good initial step in addressing them in life.

One other suggestion in line with such honesty is that we consider being as detailed as possible in our prayers. Often in prayer our gratitude is too general and our repentance too vague. This is also the case with intercessory prayer. If someone is sick or has lost a job we would probably mention it when we were with other friends. We should do the same when with God. Also, if we say to someone we will pray for him or her, then let's write this promise down and pray for that person at least once specifically *by name*. This makes our relationships with others, our prayer, and thus our relationship with God more real.

Formal prayers are also important. But we may want to supplement the ones we learned in childhood with some of the psalms, new prayers, or ones we have created on our own. Prayers we create on our own can be modeled after ones we now love or read that others have created. They can of course also be created on our own without copying the structure of another prayer. However, the important thing, as in the case of conversations with God, is that they are realistic and sound like us. Otherwise, they will sound and be phony—which is a far cry from the kind of prayers we hear from the psalmists or Jesus, whose words of prayer come from their hearts.

Rabbi Lionel Blue once said that Jews "are not holy asparagus growing to the heavens...they are noisy when they pray."[9] We too should have this kind of passion when we pray to our creator—the same kind of passion we would want to share with our parents or best friends when we felt deeply about something.

Reflections during the day are also a good way to build up one's prayer life. In addition they help us to be more present to what is happening to us in the "now." Someone once said that "Life is something that happens to us while we are busy doing something else." A reflective attitude toward life helps us to not be lost in our musings or asleep to the possibilities in life. Furthermore, it is not hard to do.

It only takes a few seconds to stop, breathe, and image yourself with God. As well as during work, it can be done in the car, when walking from one place to another, or waiting on a line in the bank. I also encourage people to image themselves as they believe God truly created them and reflect on how they are acting and interacting during the day based on this image.

In my case, the image sometimes is of someone who is hopeful and encouraging of others. When I see this image it helps me to be more gentle and accepting of others, to inspire rather than dominate conversations, and to see how I can model hope in how I live my life.

Periods of *silence and solitude* during the day are also essential. When asked for the most basic suggestion I can give about prayer, I always say the same thing: "Take two minutes out each morning in silence and solitude, wrapped in gratitude before the Lord." When I get looks that say, "Is that all?" I respond with the look, "You don't lie to me and I won't lie to you. You have been promising more time for years and rarely are you faithful to it."

If more time is desired and taken, fine. But a *minimum* of two minutes each day is essential to center oneself, know who one is, and move into the day with a sense of true identity.

The whole process is very simple. Find a quiet spot in the house. If your house is crowded, stay in bed a bit longer or use the time during your morning shower. In this space center yourself on God by using a word (Abba, Love, Friend, God, Mother...), a line from scripture, or by first reading a few words from a spirituality book. Then, image yourself being covered with the clear comforting Light of God and simply remain quiet for a few minutes in the presence of God. That's it. Nothing to achieve. Nothing to do. Just be with the Lord before the day gets going.

Spending longer times alone in silence and solitude is also obviously of benefit. The British poet Anne Shaw once said that "Fond as we are of our loved ones, there comes a time during their absence of an unexplained peace."[10]

It is my belief that silence and solitude can even improve our relations with our loved ones as well as with many others in our life. For when we have contemplative periods, there are opportunities for us to drop our defenses, games, and "neediness" so we can reach out to others in a clearer, more welcoming fashion.

During these periods we also learn the importance of being responsible in life as well as recognizing situations when we are being over-responsible (what some people would refer to as "co-dependent"). In the quiet of time alone with the Lord our consciousness clears and creates a psychological vacuum, which is then filled by our preconscious (that area of consciousness just below the surface of our awareness which contains our denials, avoidances, games, repressions, suppressions, and doubts).

When these elements come up and face us, we are able to then see how we have avoided responsibility by being either irresponsible or over-responsible. Being responsible actually involves our going through five stages (although we might not recognize it at the time). With prayer in silence and solitude we will be called to steps four and five which we sometimes don't take, thus resulting in pain for us and others. Those five steps are:

1. Recognize a problem;

2. Diagnose the real source of the problem;

3. Plan on how to deal with it;

4. Do something about it; and

5. Once we have done what we can, *let God take care of the residue.*

Acting on what we know we should do and handing over to God what we can't control isn't easy. However, being with God in silence and solitude can help us see the need for steps 4 and 5 more clearly. It can also help us recognize those instances when we avoid doing them. It is during periods of solitude with God that we have a chance for reassessment of our lives and can practice asking God for help in enlightening us. So, rather than this period being a time for escape or hiding in our shells like turtles, it is a time for us to embrace honesty, courage, and a chance for freshness of mind and openness of heart.

Spiritual writing is also a helpful way to pray. Many people are earnest, dedicated, faithful journalers. That's lovely. For others like myself, the process is a bit more haphazard or indirect. For instance, at the end of the day I like to take a few minutes to write down quotes from books I have read, stories I have heard, or reflections I have had. These bits of information not only say things about the people and places from where I got them, but also about me, since I found them of import.

Some other good things about having a notebook or folder in which we put our daily or weekly reflections are:

The activity of spiritual writing is one which removes us from a world of competition and comparisons. Journaling is by and for us;

Because we often forget fleeting but significant feelings and thoughts, journaling (or "spiritual letter-writing" as I prefer to call it) provides a clear detailed record while the impressions are clear;

Moving into the future requires that we know what we have done in the past so we can employ learning in the present. This is difficult when we have no record of our progress—or lack of it;

Writing allows us to see what we are thinking and feeling, so it encourages us to summarize and internalize our understandings better. (One member of the U.S. Congress was asked what he felt was the greatest challenge facing the U.S. Senate today, and he said: "Not enough time to think." Journaling is another way to provide us with this time for reflection); and

Spiritual letter writing helps us to see connections and themes so we can learn from the deep center of ourselves that can come to the fore during the quiet process of recollection and writing.

Journaling or letter-writing from our heart to the heart of God based on the activities of the day, then, is a wonderful way to enrich our prayer lives.[11]

Creating your own parables is yet another wonderful prayerful activity. On the surface such a process might seem a bit foreboding, or people might not be sure what I mean by this. The undertaking is quite simple, though. Parables or stories simply involve our creating a tale in which we interact with God in some way around a hope, issue, theme, or event which is at the heart of our lives at this point.

Creating stories is actually quite easy. Children love to do it and get right into the process. For example, one little boy was read the story of the Annunciation from Luke's Gospel. He was then asked to make believe he was Jesus asking the Angel Gabriel (who was to be played by a little girl in his class) to go down and appear to Mary. He gave brilliant instructions on what she was to do and ended them with the statement: "Now remember, be nice to Mary because I want her to be my mother." I think he and everyone who heard the story got new insight into the Annunciation from this simple retelling of the story.

By creating a story in which the Lord and we are involved with some issue or question that is pressing in our lives now, a number of potentially good results can occur. These include our coming to greater clarity around:

How we image God;

How we feel God sees us at this point;

What the most important elements in our life which we would like to bring to God's (and our own) attention are; and

Where we see God's activity in our lives.

To create our own parable, a number of simple suggestions might help the process be more fruitful and less cumbersome. *First,* picture a physical setting in which you want the story to take place and be as imaginative as you can. *Second,* keep the number of characters involved to a minimum so the story doesn't get too complex. *Third,* consider a theme that you want to be present in the story. *Fourth,* as you create the story in your mind and say it out loud or tape record/write it down, be as specific and imaginative as possible. In other words, put yourself in the scene and picture it as vividly as possible.

You may not feel that you are imaginative, but most people are surprised when they undertake the creation of a parable. It is actually quite enjoyable and cathartic to ventilate our feelings and concerns.

Once the parable is created, if you feel comfortable with doing so, it is also a good idea to share it with some people you trust to see their reaction. In one case, for instance, when I shared what I experienced, the person with me responded by telling me what she felt was truly accurate spiritually and theologically. She also shared with me what she believed came from my own fears and limited sense of God. Finally, she was able to ask me what I planned to do about my life now that I had reflected on my relationship with God in this way—a good question to ask after you have developed such a story.

To provide an illustration, I shall close this brief chapter on praying and the interior life with a sample parable. As you read it, please put yourself in my place where you can and take some time to see how you feel after having read it.

~ *The Meeting* ~

A Parable

As soon as I stepped in the forest, I knew I'd be sorry. It was a lot cooler than I thought. The bright morning summer sun had fooled me when I looked out the window earlier. But it was too late to go back for a heavy long-sleeved shirt or a sweater. He might be gone if I delayed any longer. I'd just have to be cold; it wouldn't kill me and the day would warm up soon enough.

After rushing along the path for about five minutes, I finally slowed down when I arrived near the spot where I thought he might be. It wouldn't be a very auspicious beginning to come crashing into the place where he sat at prayer. And since I am sometimes quite clumsy, I needed to make an extra effort so I wouldn't disturb him.

Slowing my pace down when I did was ideally timed. For after walking about one hundred feet further I saw him sitting quietly praying in the distance. Looking around, I saw a flat-topped tree stump. It was probably cut by someone assigned to clean up the dead debris after one of the powerful storms that had recently come through the area. With my handkerchief I wiped the dew off it as best as I could, sat down, and waited for him to be done.

Thank goodness I brought a full thermos of hot coffee to drink or I would have really been chilled through to the bone. Slowly I unscrewed the top and poured myself a cup of black rich coffee. (At home I usually "snow" the coffee with great amounts of milk and sugar. But when I am in the forest, I always drink it

31

black to somehow match the simplicity and straightfor-
wardness of the woods themselves.)

After about ten minutes, he slowly got up, turned
around and, squinting into the distance, saw me watch-
ing him. For a moment I was worried about what his
reaction might be at this possible intrusion on my part.
But as soon as the anxiety registered in my mind, it was
melted by a broad smile that seemed to say: "Well, what
a nice surprise!"

He walked straight toward me and ducked under a
low hanging branch just in front of the clearing in
which I sat. He quickly relaxed on another stump
across from me. And, after crossing his legs and rub-
bing his face with his left hand, he asked: "Do you have
enough coffee for me too?"

Surprised (I had forgotten I had brought the coffee
with me), I nodded, quickly cleaned out the thermos top
with a tissue, filled it, and handed him a steaming hot
cup. Finally, after taking two sips, he smiled and said
both gently and almost matter-of-factly, "Well, how may
I be of help to you?"

Quickly I launched through a thumbnail sketch of
where I felt I was in life. As I did this I was secretly hop-
ing I would have a chance to get some guidance before
the women and men who came with him last night
awoke and looked for him. However, while I spoke I
noticed that he listened quietly and attentively—as if I
were the only person in the world.

When I had finished what I wanted to say, he
seemed to be taking measure of me and my story.
Finally, he said: "You seem to be doing some good
things in your life. You are pretty faithful to a life of
prayer and recollection each day, and you outlined well
the dangers in trying to live a life that has some real

meaning in it. However, from what you tell me, something seems to be missing.

"*Nothing you are doing seems filled with the kind of deep quiet passion you'd like. You're busy and stressed one minute, and bored and drifting the next. It sounds as if you'd like some way to grasp a clear faith-filled way to live your life.*"

"*Yes,*" *I said quickly.*

"*Well,*" *he said, "I can offer you a few things to reflect on and pray about that should be helpful. They will not remove the darkness and confusion but instead help you to live within it for now and learn what it can teach you. Since this doesn't exactly answer the questions you came with, do you still want what I have to offer you?*"

"*Yes, Lord, I do.*"

"*Well, then...*

.....

Liken yourself to a beautiful original part of creation—a true work of art. Then each day ask yourself how you are living either in ways that show gratitude for this beauty or in ways that indicate how you are defacing it.

Read a little scripture each week to see what I have said to others searching for the Truth like you. In this way you may learn from the past in order to know better which way to step in the future.

Continue to do some simple things for others in need and look for my presence as you do these little good works.

And finally, take quiet time each morning to remember me and our time together.

.....

"Will you do this?"

"I will, Lord."

Then, as I was answering, he got up and walked over to me. Standing next to me he smiled again, took off his flannel shirt, wrapped it around me, and squeezed my shoulder gently with his right hand. Finally, he said: "I will remember you." He then disappeared from sight to leave me with some of the doubts in my heart gone for now but with more questions than ever burning inside as to the direction I should go and the decisions I had to make each day in light of this encounter.

Yet, somehow the questions and doubts didn't seem to be the same as before. Instead, they just sat there alongside me in the forest as new friends I just needed to get to know better.

Finally, I too got up. And when I did, I realized I was no longer so cold anymore, so I took off my new flannel shirt and folded it gently over my arm. Then I began to slowly walk back home while enjoying the late morning sun.

I felt it was going to be a beautiful new day.

Amen.

II

Caring

I don't know what your destiny will be,
but one thing I know,
the only ones among you who will be really
happy are those who have sought and found
how to serve.

—Albert Schweitzer[12]

Just as praying to God is a foundation of the spiritual life, so is caring for others. The fine Jewish theologian Martin Buber put it well when he said: "He who loves brings God and the world together."

So many people are in such pain today. So many people are suffering and are in need of our understanding and support. But the questions remain: How can we do this in today's stressful world? What would a caring attitude involve for a person who wishes to embrace a full spiritual life?

To answer this, it is probably a good idea to know not only what caring is but also what it is *not:*

> Being available to others is not just giving time, money, and effort. It is also not endlessly worrying about others so that our personal tension rises to the point that we are overloaded and have no energy to care about anything or anyone else. After all, what would such imprudent masochism prove? Instead, being really available to others is being creatively alive for, and with, them. The true goal, which unfortunately often gets distorted or lost, is to share the Lord

with others while in turn looking for and enjoying his sometimes almost-hidden presence as it
is revealed in them.[13]

And so, caring is "not in saying a lot of words to people, not in completing a compulsive list of works, and not
in trying to respond to everyone's expectations (includ-
ing our own!), but in trying, with all of our being, to
develop an attitude of openness and alertness in our interactions with others which is based on only one thing: the
desire to look for and bring God *everywhere.*"[14] And a
cornerstone of such a wonderful form of caring is the
beautiful gift of *presence.*

The Gift of Presence

How we are *with* people is probably the most ele-
gant part of caring. The following story poignantly illustrates the simplicity of this:

One day a woman's little girl arrived home late
after school. The mother was so angry that she
started to yell at her. However, after about five
minutes, she suddenly stopped and asked:
"Why are you so late anyway?"
The daughter replied: "Because I had to help
another girl who was in trouble."
"Well, what did you do to help her?"
The daughter replied: "Oh, I sat down next to
her and helped her cry."[15]

The value of presence to another person should not
be understated. When we sit with people in the darkness
and "help them cry" we model hope and new possibilities in ways even we sometimes don't realize.

A wonderful woman who had been through a good

deal of trauma early in her life was pure joy to experience in the final months of her therapy. She was playful, filled with wonder about her own creative abilities, and generous in her friendship with the many others who turned to her for support because of her boundless vitality.

As I watched this, I wanted her to reflect on the difference between her experience of herself now and how she saw herself earlier in life. The goal was to help her see the process of rediscovery so it could be applied again and again in life. Also, I wanted her to rejoice in the progress she had made; she had worked very hard during her time with me.

So I asked her: "How do you understand the difference between how you are now and how you were earlier in life? Then you seemed so shut up inside. Now you tell me you enjoy your playfulness, creativeness, and the joining of the woman you are now with the child within you that once seemed so lost. How have you done it?"

She looked at me quite puzzled and finally said: "You mean you really don't know?"

"No, I don't," I replied.

She then said: "It was simple. I just watched the way you interacted with me and I started treating myself in the same way."

"Presence" is truly one of the best gifts we can offer to others in need.

The Necessary Pain

Caring also involves a degree of necessary pain. As one rabbi said many years ago: "When you reach down to help others who have fallen into a ditch, you have to be prepared to get a little dirty yourself."

This lesson is sometimes a hard one to learn. And, even for those of us who are educated about this as professional helpers, the dangers are still always present. At some level, no matter how much care is taken to keep an appropriate sense of distance, still, one feels the chill of the darkness in people's lives. No one who really cares is immune. This is even so when the situation turns out to be a hopeful one filled with possibility and beneficial results.

One gifted person who visited with me weekly a few years back said to me toward the end of our time together: "I thought of the times I had reflected on the gift of our relationship and how I liked to say, 'We both laugh, but I'm the only one who cries.' And it came to me that this was not really true. The reality is that you also cry, but mysteriously and sacrificially because you do so inwardly." Her statement was very perceptive.

In fourth century Persia we hear one desert father warn the others that if you see someone sinking in quicksand, do *not* reach out a hand but instead first grab a stick lest you both be pulled down. To care today, we must take note of this warning. When we care we must be willing to be open to receiving support ourselves. A community of friends is not a nicety in the spiritual life of a caring person—it is a necessity!

Listening

In addition to appreciating the value of "presence" and having an awareness of the realistic toll we must sometimes pay in reaching out to others in need, a caring attitude also, at its very core, involves embracing a special kind of *willingness.* By that I mean:

—A willingness to *listen;*

—A willingness to *be open;* and

—A willingness to *be faithful.*

All three serve to enrich our sense of compassion as well as to minimize the frustration we may encounter. And first among them is the simple ability to *listen.*

Being genuine is tough today. In our public relations–oriented society, there is really no market for ordinariness. As a result, we often feel we should be better or different from what we are; we also may overestimate our errors, failures, shames, and blemishes, and then hide accordingly. I think that it is only when persons who are also spiritual listen to our whole story and embrace us that we become really free. In turn, in experiencing our own sense of self-worth we can then offer this same gift to others by how we relate to them.

The following story is one a student shared with me about herself after one of my classes on the spirituality of self-acceptance. She asked me to tell it to others if I thought it would be of help. I tell it now because I think it illustrates beautifully the wonderful value of allowing people to tell their stories and shows how important *real* listening, acceptance, and responding from the heart are to others.

When she was only a young vowed religious, Sister was sent as a missioner to Africa. When she was preparing for the trip, she was very excited about the ministry she thought she would be doing, only to be told when she arrived that her work would be teaching science in one of the local secondary schools.

Discouraged by this type of work, she cheered up a few months later when the local bishop asked her to help prepare an elderly couple to enter the church. Since this is what she originally supposed she would be doing, the thought of even starting in a little way to do such a ministry was pure joy to her.

When she started the catechetical work with the couple, the woman, who had two brothers but no sisters, started to really warm up to her. However, she also began to put Sister up on a pedestal.

The Sister felt good about the relationship and valued it deeply but became increasingly alarmed because of the totally positive way she was being viewed. Finally she decided to do something about it. What she decided to do was to tell the woman the most embarrassing and shameful thing she could think of about herself.

So, the next time she came to visit the woman in her little one-room house, she sat on the opposite side of the bed from her (since there were no chairs there) and started telling her the tale she wished to share. Half-way through the telling the Sister became quite fearful, thinking: "What if this destroys the relationship?"

Finally, after she finished the story she held her breath, convinced by now that telling the story was the most foolish thing she could have done. Certainly, she thought, this has surely destroyed the magic of our relationship.

*After a short pause, the woman got up, came around the bed, and gave the Sister a big hug and said: "Thank you for having told me this." And seeing the concern still in Sister's eyes, she added in a soft voice: "Don't you understand? Now that you have told me this I don't love you less. I love you **more**."*

When the Sister left that small house later in the afternoon she felt freed and thought: "Now, I don't care what anyone thinks or knows about me. It just doesn't matter."

This is the possible result of allowing people to tell their *total* story to us when we are willing to offer them unconditional acceptance. What happens during such an encounter is that we open the door for them to experience a reflection of the same spiritual acceptance God gives us—and what could be more of a blessing than this?

A primary goal of listening then is to help persons (and ourselves for that matter) to see everything simply and truthfully. When this occurs it is very liberating if people also feel simultaneously valued and accepted. But secular society hides from such simplicity and honesty, and because of this, communication suffers and people often fail to simply say what they know to be true.

Children can teach us clarity and simplicity when we interact with them. We need only watch them or listen to their stories to have this borne out.

For instance, when a daughter of a fellow parishioner of mine was five years old, her older sister (who was a freshman in college at the time) invited her to spend the weekend with her at college. Toward the end of the weekend together, one of the older sister's roommates complimented the child in her sister's presence by saying: "She's the most precocious child I've ever met."

The older sister looked at her younger sister and said: "You don't know what that means, do you?"

"Yes I do," the younger sister replied. "It means I do and say things you don't expect me to do at my age."

Quite taken aback, the older sister asked: "Well, how ever did you know that?"

And the child replied quite simply: "Because I'm precocious!"[16]

As the poet Jean Cocteau once said: "The poet doesn't invent. He listens." Children and caring adults who try not to interject their many hidden agendas are able to do the same.

Too often we feel we must have all the answers to

the questions and needs people express. Unfortunately, because of this attitude not only our listening but also our communication becomes stifled. As a result, the interactions between us and others seem like two ships passing in the night.

One bishop illustrated this when he told the following story about himself visiting an area nursing home:

When he entered the foyer of the home he saw a woman originally from his parish, but he didn't note recognition of him in her eyes when she looked his way. So, he walked over to her and said: "Do you know who I am?"

She answered: "No, but it's all right. The same thing happens to me all the time. Just walk over to that woman at the desk and she will be able to tell you."

One of the reasons listening is a rare gift today is that so many of us (possibly because of our anxiety) strive too hard to do something useful or to be immediately helpful in some tangible way. The problem is that in the process of doing this we fail to really listen to a person's pain. In becoming stressed out ourselves over what we need to do to be "successful" with someone in need, we often fail to realize the pure value that listening in and of itself is. Furthermore, when we're not observing the situation for what it really is, we not only miss a chance for understanding, but occasionally may even make the situation worse by acting too impulsively.

For instance, a man once looked through his window and saw his neighbor's car slowly rolling out of the driveway next door with no one at the wheel. He quickly jumped into action, ran out of his house, leaped into the car, and jammed on the emergency brake.

Then, coming out of the car, feeling the satisfaction of having helped avert a near disaster, he screamed with joy: "I stopped it!"

To which his neighbor who was walking around from behind the vehicle replied sullenly: "I know. I was pushing it!"[17]

Listening, *in and of itself,* says that I:

—Really care;

—Truly want to know you better;

—Am willing to spend the time and energy to try to understand your situation;

—Will provide reflection, feedback, and questions to see if we both see the issues clearly; and

—Am willing to work with you on gaining new perspectives on the problems and questions at hand.

Listening helps both the person telling the story and the other individual present to receive and examine from different vantage points the narratives being shared. Listeners don't passively hear but instead expend a great deal of energy trying to open up a story. People are often trapped by the narrowness of their own stories. With spiritual friends though one can look at those stories from different angles so as to enlarge their possibilities by seeing what they have shared, and who they are, from *a different perspective.*

Openness to New Perspectives

Our outlook can dramatically impact our whole angle of vision. What we refer to as "our perspective" helps us to view things, situations, other people, even *ourselves* in a

unique way. Brother John Beeching, a Maryknoll mission-
ary I met in Thailand, points this out in the following
experience he had while he was in the Mideast:

> Some years ago, I was assigned to work in Egypt.
> My work took me across the city of Cairo every
> day on a three-car trolley. Although the street
> cars all appeared identical, one was designated
> as "first class" and charged a slightly higher fare.
> I finally asked a fellow passenger to explain
> what made the difference. After a protracted
> pause, he said, "It is true that the cars are the
> same, but the difference between first and sec-
> ond class is *what you think of yourself.*"

As well as the view we have of ourselves, even bad
news can be changed by what perspective we have. A
number of years ago I had a colleague who like myself was
adding the few unwanted pounds that represent one of
the "gifts" of middle age. Then, after having missed seeing
him for about a month, I met him again at the copying
machine and saw that he was much thinner (which was
very disconcerting because I still had my weight on)!

I said to him: "How could you do this to me? Lose
weight so now I am fat by myself?"

The curious reply he gave me in a subdued voice
was: "Ah, I need to talk to you about that. Will you be up
in your office in a few minutes?" What started out as our
usual repartee now seemed quite ominous from the tone
in his voice.

As I sat in my office waiting for him to show up, I
thought all kinds of terrible things. For instance, one
thought that flashed through my mind at the time was:
"He must have advanced cancer or something awful to
cause him to lose that weight so quickly." I didn't know

what to think. Finally, by the time he arrived *I* was anxious and completely stressed out myself.

After coming into my office, he sat down and calmly said, "I think I'm going to lose my job." In response, rather than being supportive to him during this difficult time in life, I had all I could do to stop myself from blurting out: "Is that all? I thought you were dying!"

I think openness to perspective is so dramatic because it loosens people up to let go of information they have held onto so as to welcome new useful material. In this way it is possible to broaden their ways of viewing themselves and the world. But letting go of old ways of thinking in order to reach out for new ways of understanding, perceiving and knowing is a little like letting go of one trapeze to grasp on to another. In such an exercise you have to leap blindly into mid-air to get to the new spot you want to reach.

And so, even when we know we are wrong, sometimes we are tempted to avoid seeing this reality clearly so we don't have to change. Consequently, at times we may be like the minister who yells the loudest when he knows the least.

We may also resist change because we have spent so much energy going in one direction that to move in another seems to be an embarrassment. I remember one cartoon of animals moving in a long line two by two onto a boat that was obviously supposed to be Noah's Ark. In the following frame two giraffes were standing tightly squeezed in next to each other sweating under a hot summer sun. Finally, in the final frame one of the giraffes says: "After all this grief, I sure to heck hope it at least rains a little." As necessary as it is, changing our present view of things, after a lot of effort has been expended to support it, is just not an easy thing to do.

Another reason we resist seeing things differently is based on the fear of what a new perspective might do to the person we know as ourself. The time-worn question is, "If I give up my present perspective, defenses and styles of dealing with the world or identity, who will I become?" The deep-seated fear is that I'll cease to exist.

We sometimes see this fear in adult survivors of sexual abuse. As awakening occurs after remembering the abuse, they see the persona they have built because of having been victimized early in life. They know they must now let go of this self-image, but the question is, Who will they be after they have achieved a new degree of healing and freedom? Fortunately, once they have been shepherded along the journey of recovery they can see some light at the end of the tunnel. Finally, as they experience more and more being in a better place in life, both the spontaneity of the little child that was hidden for so long joins with the power of a new-found assertive adult to produce a beautiful person of the Spirit.

Anthony de Mello in his lecture tours used to address the fear of embracing a new identity by using the following example:

> Suppose somebody walks into my room one day. I say, "Come right in. May I know who you are?" And he says, "I am Napoleon." And I say, "Not the Napoleon..." And he says, "Precisely. Bonaparte, Emperor of France." "What do you know!" I say, even while I'm thinking to myself, "I better handle this guy with care." "Sit down, Your Majesty," I say. "Well, they tell me you're a pretty good spiritual director. I have a spiritual problem. I'm anxious; I'm finding it hard to trust in God. I have my armies in Russia, see, and I'm spending sleepless

nights wondering how it's going to turn out." So I say, "Well, Your Majesty, I could certainly prescribe something for that. What I suggest is that you read chapter 6 of Matthew: "Consider the lilies of the field...they neither toil nor spin."

By this point I'm wondering who is crazier, this guy or me. But I go along with [him]. That's what the wise guru does with you in the beginning. He goes along with you...[However,] the time has to come soon when he'll pull the rug out from under your feet and tell you, "Get off it, you're not Napoleon."...[And] when the man comes to his senses and realizes he is not Napoleon, he does not cease to be. He continues to be, but suddenly realizes that he is something other than what he thought he was.[18]

The same is the case with us and those whom we seek to befriend in life. When we gain new perspectives the opportunity arrives through which we can live a little more and find out a bit better who we really are in the eyes of God. And this is certainly preferable to resisting change. For, as Anne Morrow Lindberg once said, "There is nothing so implacably punished by nature than resistance to change."[19]

The problem is too often we don't realize how rigid our thinking is until it is too late:

Once a village blacksmith found an apprentice willing to work hard at low pay. The smith immediately began his instructions to the young fellow: "When I take the metal out of the fire, I'll lay it on the anvil; and when I nod my head you hit it with the hammer." The apprentice did precisely what *he thought* he was told.

Next day *he* was the village blacksmith!

Openness to new perspectives also allows us to aid others to see what was previously deemed unhelpful information by them in new valuable ways. For instance, one depressed student after the loss of his mother told me: "I study hard only because I am too embarrassed to get a low grade." My response to him was, "Your studying hard is the seed of new possibility. Though you play down the value of your motivation for doing it, the studying is an example of 'silent hope.' Since activity and depression don't like to live together, your work, no matter what the motivation underlying it is now, is still something good in your life."

Openness to new perspectives also requires *us* in our caring roles to be willing to see things differently. Two occasions come to mind when this was brought across to me quite clearly.

One was in the early years of my clinical practice when an old monk was sent to see me by his community. At the designated time of his first appointment, I went out to meet him in the waiting room and extended my hand to greet him. When I did this, he looked up and gave me a dirty look. And I said to him: "Good grief, Brother, you are giving me dirty looks and I haven't even begun the treatment yet." His response was, "That's why they sent me to you!"

At that point I invited him to come into my office (because you can't charge people for counseling done in the waiting room). And after seeing him for a while I realized that he wasn't suffering from "an angry heart." Instead, he was suffering from a broken one (which he had been protecting up to this point through the use of anger). If it weren't for our time together and my willingness to get to know him, I would have thought like others that he was simply stubborn and angry and would have missed so much about this wonderful talented man. In turn, if I hadn't been willing to look further as to why he was behaving in an angry fashion, I wouldn't have been able to help him adjust to the changes in the church which he found so threatening.

The second example is one in which I required a bit more prodding to gain an appropriate perspective. With this person I needed additional help to see how I had completely missed the point—and the help to see this wound up coming from the very person who was coming to me for assistance. This person was very perceptive and energetic and a pleasure to work with on the process of self-understanding and self-discovery.

In the encounter in question, she came in for one of our meetings and said: "You know, I have thought and thought about what you told me last time we were together and I still don't get it." After repeating to me the interpretation I had made at the end of our last session together, she then asked: "Do you think your comment was more of a 'male thing' and doesn't really apply to me, or did I miss the point?"

After thinking about it for a bit, I realized she was right. I was coming from a very male-oriented perspective and I said with a bit of hesitation: "Yes, I guess it was a male thing on my part."

She took this admission very matter of factly and said: "Oh, all right. I just didn't want to waste a lot of additional time if it was *your* issue and not mine," and continued on by discussing the topic she wished to address that day. An amazing woman.

And so, when it comes to openness to new perspectives, as caring persons we have to be the *first* to model it through a willingness to admit we are wrong. Otherwise, we are teaching one thing and modeling another.

Faithfulness

Finally, in looking at caring we turn to the essential trait of "faithfulness." When people seek our caring presence, in addition to listening and an openness to new perspectives, faithfulness is also crucial. But, although we may know and accept this, faithfulness to people who are in pain, depressed, under stress, or experiencing a great loss is never easy. This is so even when we feel pretty certain that God is calling us to be with that person. For as Elie Wiesel once stated (in a way probably only he could): "When you see an angel of the Lord coming with the words 'Be not afraid,' you know you're in trouble!"

Faithfulness is a rare commodity today. When the going gets tough for us, we sometimes tend to think of running as the first meaningful exercise in which to engage.

Our faithfulness cannot rely on the gratefulness, compliance, or results we see in, or receive from, others. If we feel that we need people to be thankful, then surely our efforts won't last long. Furthermore, if we expect that people will actually always follow all of our suggestions, then we are in even greater trouble!

Faithfulness instead must rely on our deep belief that the very act of caring is worthwhile. This is hope in action. In one of my favorite quotes from the book *Compassion* by McNeil, Morrison and Nouwen, this point is well made:

> Here we are touching the profound spiritual
> truth that service is an expression of the search
> for God and not just of the desire to bring about

social change. This is open to all sorts of misunderstandings, but its truth is confirmed in the lives of those for whom service is a constant and uninterrupted concern. As long as the help we offer to others is motivated primarily by the changes we may accomplish, our service cannot last long. When results do not appear, when success is absent, when we are no longer liked or praised for what we do, we lose the strength and motivation to continue. When we see nothing but sad, poor, sick, or miserable people who, even after our many attempts to offer help, remain sad, poor, sick, and miserable, then the only reasonable response is to move away in order to prevent ourselves from becoming cynical or depressed. Radical servanthood challenges us, while attempting persistently to overcome poverty, hunger, illness, and any other form of human misery, to reveal the gentle presence of our compassionate God in the midst of our broken world.[20]

Faithfulness then is modeling ourselves after the Lord who has been and remains worthy of our trust. Faithfulness is a way of saying to the world that I believe in God's goodness no matter what sadness or cruelty I see. Just as it is a beautiful gift to us in our own covenant with God, faithfulness is also one of the greatest gifts we can give to others.

Final Comments on Caring

If we pray over the themes of listening, openness to new perspectives, and faithfulness, maybe we can enable our caring presence to be more gentle, honest, and strong. Any techniques learned during life which help us care are important, but the essential step is *to simply care.*

I tend to agree with Aldous Huxley who said: "It is a bit embarrassing to have been concerned all one's life and find that at the end one has no more to offer by way of advice than: *Try to be a little kinder.*" It is this basic willingness to gently reach out which is at the basis of all caregiving.

Also, hopefully by better incorporating the attitudes presented in this chapter, we can begin as well to see a little more that in caring for others, God is in some mysterious way caring for us. Accordingly, this may help us to recall more often, when we are with others, to "try to be a little kinder."

The following closing prayer for this chapter is meant to reflect and encourage just such an outlook and desire.

~ *Let Me Remember* ~

O gentle and caring God...

When I feel frustrated by someone's ingratitude and
seemingly impossible expectations,
>*let me remember* his neediness or fear of saying
>"Thanks."

When I face a person's rage,
>*let me remember* the pain she has long endured at
>the hands of many others so I can
>give her the space to share her anger freely and with-
>out fear.

When someone sees the world (and me) in extreme negative and positive ways,
>*let me remember* that I am neither the devil...nor,
>for that matter, am I God.

When people are very troubled and I begin to feel over-
whelmed by it all too,
>*let me remember* that "simply listening" is truly a
>quiet, great grace in itself.

And, when I see a person making the same mistakes over
and over again,
>*let me remember* that sometimes I'm not such a
>winner myself!

Yes, as I sit with others who are sad, in pain, under stress,
depressed, anxious and afraid,
>*let me remember* your gentle faithfulness,
>so I can be present to others in the same way you
>always are to me.

Amen.

—Robert J. Wicks

III

Nurturing

The problem of our youth is not youth. The problem is the spirit of our age: denial of transcendence, the vapidity of values, emptiness in the heart, the decreased sensitivity to the imponderable quality of the spirit...The central problem is that we do not know how to think, how to pray, how to cry, how to resist the deceptions of too many persuaders.[21]

—Abraham Joshua Heschel

I think that any man who watches three football games in a row should be declared legally dead.[22]

—Erma Bombeck

Just as the taste for good music, food, and art doesn't develop overnight, so neither does the ability to spend our wisdom years in a rich, full, and gracious way. And so, we need to take care to fill our hearts with activities or events that give life rather than being mesmerizing. In addition, the importance of having a series of good ways to appreciate life helps us avoid one of the greatest dangers of the spiritual life: "*acedia,*" the "noontime demon" or "spiritual boredom," as this state is variously termed.

People often think that once bad habits, addictions, unnecessary fears, worries, anger, anxiety, and stress are gone, a state of peace will follow. But although peace does come with such a removal of *unnecessary* distress (because all of us will always have a degree of necessary pain in our lives), the problem Jesus cited in telling the following story can occur as well:

> When the unclean spirit has gone out of a person, it wanders through waterless regions looking for a resting place, but it finds none. Then it says, "I will return to my house from which I came." When it comes, it finds it empty, swept, and put in order. Then it goes and brings along seven other spirits more evil than itself, and they enter and live there; and the last state of that person is worse than the first. (Mt 12:43-45)

Tocqueville, a French political figure, traveler, historian and social critic who lived in the 1800s, once said that: "The most dangerous time for a bad government is when it starts to reform itself." I think the same can be said of people—even people who are not "bad" as such but, like most of us, are sometimes misguided and misdirected yet still willing to claim their addictions, poor habits, and ingrained maladaptive styles for what they are. However, when we and they have let go of obviously wrong behavior or addictions, what then? Even when we seem to be living a fairly good life we must still face the question: If we don't fill our souls with behavior and stimulation that is bad, with what will we fill it?

Not to do anything may be tantamount to inviting trouble. Owning our sins is only the first step. For as a character in one of Trevanian's novels said: "Confession is good for the spirit...it empties the soul making more space for sin."[23]

So, once again the question is, What is needed so the old bad habits are not replaced by new more potent ones? Well, maybe there is an indirect tip to be had from another novel, Daniel Easterman's *The Ninth Buddha.* In it the comment is made about a young person that "He was too young to understand that sin was just as much a part of life as prayer, or that holiness, like water, would grow stagnant if it was allowed to lie too long without being stirred."[24]

The answer is: We need to be stirred! We need to be nourished. We need new manna to fill our genuine needs for nourishment. Otherwise, addictions, old habits, worrying, and a need for excitement will step in to fill the void of boredom.

Such "manna" to nurture our spiritual life appears in a myriad of ways and is probably more plentiful than we realize. For our purposes here, though, I would like to suggest the following to start our thinking about how we should seek out spiritual nourishment: *reading; friend-ship; good projects and activities;* and *leisurely walks.* My hope is that these suggestions will seed further ideas and activities that offer nourishment for the soul.

Reading

Dorothy Day, the founder of the *Catholic Worker,* was once commiserating with an alcoholic. The woman sitting with her said that she actually had to close her eyes when she walked past a bar so she wouldn't be tempted to go inside. Dorothy Day retorted to this: "I know what you mean. I have to do the same when I pass a bookstore."

Many of us are like this ourselves—especially now in the age of megabookstores with music sections and coffee shops. Now, instead of the usual cry, "Let's go to the mall," we often suggest to one another, "Why don't we go to a bookstore, browse, and have some coffee?" However, even though more and more of us go to bookstores, many of us still don't really read enough. Moreover, even if we do, we probably don't read enough of what would help us develop sufficiently as caring, loving, challenging persons.

Joe Ciarrocchi is a wonderful and warm colleague of mine at Loyola College. (He is also author of the two very helpful Paulist Press books *Why Are You Worrying?* and *The Doubting Disease*—a book on religiosity and compulsivity.) Each semester he would tease his new students about me with the statement: "My dream is to come up with a new idea about which Bob Wicks hasn't already written a book!"

When students report this comment to me (as they always do), I have the following response ready: "Well, I have a similar fantasy. I would love to read a book and be able to tell Joe about it without having him always say to me: 'Yes, I remember that book, Bob—I read it when it *first* came out a few years ago!'"

Most of us may have the natural sense of curiosity that Joe has as well as his high motivation to respond to it with a rich reading regimen. However, quite a few of us probably still need to actually take certain additional steps in order to nourish our souls with a more vibrant tapestry of material than we are availing ourselves of now.

The first step in doing this is very simple: set out time to read on a regular basis. Today, money and the provision of *time* often indicate our level of commitment to something. Joe Ciarrocchi, who is a full-time professor as well as a clinician, lecturer, family man and active researcher, finds time (or, more accurately, sets aside the necessary time) to read.

Yet, the *amount* of time is not the only important factor. Like prayer, time for reading is often set aside—in theory—in large blocks. But when the realities of our crazy schedules intervene, little if any prayer or reading is accomplished. The answer to this problem may be reasonableness rather than tenacity.

Years ago when I was an undergraduate student, the chairperson of the philosophy department and I discussed various interests. Once, when the topic of reading fiction came up, he said that he set aside twenty minutes each night for reading a novel. To this statement I made a facial expression which gave him the message: "Is that all the fiction you read?" In response to my look, he said: "Twenty minutes each night on a regular basis is a heck of a lot of fiction over the period of a year, Bob." And, of course, he was right.

The important first element in having a reading plan for ourselves so that our hearts are nourished by the ideas, themes, challenges, and hopes of others is for us to set up *regular times to read* to which we will be faithful. Once this is done, we can then address two other issues in developing a reading plan. They are *breadth* and *depth*.

Breadth and Depth

Even persons who read a great deal still run the risk of getting caught in a rut. Some of us may only read certain types of novels, a particular type of devotional material, or solely material of a certain genre. Just as in the case of our physical well-being, our spiritual health depends upon a varied and balanced "diet" of good reading. Such a diet should include: good fiction, autobiographies/biographies, journals, general non-fiction, books of quotations, poetry/books of prayers, books of contemporary and "classic" spirituality, and of course sacred scripture.

Good Fiction. In addition to the type of novels we normally enjoy, reading other types of books which challenge and open us up is a good idea. The best-seller list is not the only source of ideas for such reading—as a matter of fact, today it may even be misleading! Winners of the Booker Prize, the Pulitzer, and the National Book Award, as well as suggestions from good friends, might be better sources. The question "What good books have you read recently?" is a good one to ask of friends whose taste and commitment to a life of meaning you respect.

Autobiographies/Biographies. In the introduction to The Radcliffe Biography Series, Matina S. Horner writes: "Fine biographies give us both a glimpse of ourselves and a reflection of the human spirit. Biography illuminates history, inspires by example, and fires the imagination to life's possibilities. Good biography can create lifelong models for us. Reading about other people's experiences encourages us to persist, to face hardship, and to feel less alone. Biography tells us about choice, the power of a personal vision, and the interdependence of human life."[25]

Reading contemporary autobiographies such as Maya Angelou's *I Know Why the Caged Bird Sings* (Bantam, 1971), Etty Hillesum's *An Interrupted Life* (Pocket Books, 1985), the Dalai Lama's *Freedom in Exile* (Harper, 1991) or Thomas Merton's *Seven Storey Mountain* (Harcourt, Brace and Jovanovich, 1948) all bear out Dr. Horner's comments. Also, reading biographies such as Robert Cole's *Dorothy Day: A Radical Devotion* (Addison-Wesley, 1987) or A.N. Wilson's life of *C.S. Lewis* (Norton, 1990) brings us into the world of persons who can help us see life differently than we might, given our own limited background. The possibilities of both autobiographies and biographies, contemporary and classic, are often overlooked by many of us for more "attractive, exciting reading." Once exposed to this type of book, though, we begin to see that real adventure is entering deeply into the life of another—

especially one who faced the despair of life and didn't give in to the situation.

Journals are another way to follow the movements and nuances of people's lives. They, like biographies, also can be quite nourishing and challenging to our souls. Dag Hammarskjöld's *Markings* (Knopf, 1976), Kathleen Norris' *Dakota* (Houghton-Mifflin, 1992), Henri Nouwen's *The Genesee Diary* (Doubleday, 1981), and Thomas Merton's *A Vow of Conversation* (Farrar, Straus, and Giroux, 1993) put us in a place where we can explore, piece by piece, the thinking and reactions of individuals trying to make spiritual sense out of the daily occurrences of their lives.

Diaries help us to travel through a geography of reflection which can serve only to help deepen our own sense of healthy introspection. In addition, as we view the diaries of others, their quality of self-understanding can help us move away from morbid and mundane preoccupation with self. They can inspire us to reach out to the world instead of being drawn into a secure quietistic shell of moody self-involvement.

Books of Quotes/Short Reflections. In New York City years ago there were several wonderful authentic Swedish smorgasbords. I just loved them. Such variety! Such quality samplings! Now they are gone, and the brutal buffets of so-so samplings have replaced them throughout the city. As a matter of fact, unfortunately, such blah buffets are everywhere.

A similar scene can be observed with books of quotes. They have proliferated as people seek more and more easy ways to nourish themselves emotionally and spiritually. As a result, motivations regarding why one is seeking such a collection is an important factor in gathering up a volume of quotes for reflection.

If the goal is to sustain oneself on such volumes,

then no matter how good a choice made, one's spiritual life will be kept fairly superficial by the use of them. Yet, if books of this type are used as a way to sample wide varieties of hearts and minds and to supplement a regular reading regimen, the results can be quite wonderfully beneficial.

Selection of the type of collection is obviously as important as the place enjoying such material plays in one's reading habits. There are many superb collections of quotes/short reflections available for our use. Anthony de Mello's *One Minute Wisdom* (Doubleday, 1986) Carolyn Warner's *The Last Word* (Prentice-Hall, 1992) and *The Great Thoughts* compiled by George Seldes (Bantam, 1985) are only three that quickly come to mind, but of course there are many more. So, spending a few minutes in a bookstore skimming through selections that initially seem of interest is always a good idea before deciding on which one to buy.

Poetry Books/Books of Prayers. Most of us read only a line or two of poetry every now and then in a magazine. However, the poetry of such persons as Rilke, Yeats, Frost, or e.e. cummings can break through our fixed ways of viewing life.

Poets see life in such a pristine way that we can be borne up by them to a vantage point we might never see if it weren't for their use of language and meter.

Prayers are also like this. In much the same way they express what we can't seem to say. If you have been put off by old books of prayers, then my suggestion is to go into a religious bookstore now and ask for advice on what prayer collections to read that have come out in the past five years. I think you might well be pleasantly surprised by some of them.

Spirituality Books. Volumes specifically designed to

help us gain a deeper understanding of our connection to what and Who is greater than our own lives are obviously important as well. Known contemporary writers such as Thomas Merton, Henri Nouwen, Joyce Rupp, James Finley, Kathleen Fischer, Metropolitan Anthony of Sourozh (Anthony Bloom), Gerald May, William Barry, Abraham Heschel, and Basil Pennington are good to sample. In addition the classic works of Teresa of Avila, John of the Cross, Thérèse of Lisieux, and John Cassian as well as books such as *The Cloud of Unknowing* and *Way of the Pilgrim* are also good sources. Moving beyond one's own tradition to read from other religious traditions is also very enlightening and inspiring. Examples of this would be the *Tao Te Ching,* the *Kabbalah,* and the many fine works from non-Christian religions available in Paulist Press' Classics of Western Spirituality series.

Sacred Scriptures. Sacred scriptures also needs to be at the heart of our reading regimen. Once again, amount of time is not as relevant as regularity and the quality of attention we give to God's words to us.

Reading sacred scriptures for five or ten minutes each week may not seem like much, but how many of us do it? How many of us relax with scripture so we can be with God in a way that we can be taught, encouraged, challenged, and given a sense of peace?

I think Abraham Heschel was right when he said, "The Bible is an answer to the supreme question: *What does God demand of us?* Yet, the question has gone out of the world. God is portrayed as a man of vagueness behind a veil of enigmas, and the voice has become alien to our minds, to our hearts, to our souls. We have learned to listen to every 'I' except the 'I' of God."[26]

Sacred scripture is the story of God and of God's relationship with people. Unfortunately, these words are often treated like dusty old furniture instead of the living, proven antique vessels of truth that can free us from the chains of contemporary secular thinking.

When we read scripture with a real sense of passion, the words of wonder in it can inspire us during our different moods:

> When we are depressed, they support us;
>
> When we are filled with joy, the words can dance with us;
>
> When we are bored, they can challenge us anew to see how we have set aside God and life behind a veil of secularism, ingratitude and entitlement.

Just reading the Bible for itself and not as duty is a nourishment that can't be rivaled.

Friendship

As well as reading, another nourishing force in the spiritual life is friendship. Margaret Mead, the famous anthropologist, once said that "One of the oldest human needs is having someone to wonder where you are when you don't come home at night."[27] In my little book with Robert Hamma, *A Circle of Friends: Encountering the Caring Voices in Your Life* (Ave Maria Press, 1996), this point is appreciated and expanded upon through a discussion of four distinct types of people needed for support today: the prophet, the cheerleader, the harasser, and the guide.

In line with the material in that book, the following questions and statements might help us appreciate the tapestry of the different types of friends we have or might need:

Do I have people with whom I can simply be myself?

What type of friends do I value most? Why?

What do I feel are the main qualities of friendship?

List and briefly describe the friends who are now in my life.

Describe ones who are no longer alive or present to me now but who have made an impact on my life. Why do I think they made such a difference in my life?

Among my circle of friends, who are my personal heroes or role models?

Who are the prophets in my life? In other words, who confronts me with the question: To what voices am I responding in life?

Who help me see my relationships, mission in life, and self-image more clearly? How do they accomplish this?

Who encourage me in a genuine way through praise and a nurturing spirit?

Who tease me into gaining a new perspective when I am too preoccupied or tied up in myself?

> Who help me experience the living God in
> new ways and help me let go of stagnant
> images of the Lord as well as outmoded
> ways of praying?
>
> When and with whom do I play different
> (prophetic, supportive...) roles as a friend?
> How do people receive such interactions?

When people are distant from friends I encourage them to write to them or call. In writing we can share things in ways we are not able to do over the phone. Many years ago a friend of mine was far away for a couple of years. We corresponded and learned about each other in ways we never had in the past (and haven't since he returned).

Writing is a lost art for many people. I have tried to keep it going for myself in my journaling as well as in the letters I respond to from friends and strangers alike. Dropping someone a card or a letter does more good than the writer ever suspects. It is a great act of friendship and a beautiful way to give/receive ministry.

Mother Teresa once said, "Loneliness is the most terrible poverty."[28] It certainly is at least one of them. The sad part too is that it can be avoided in many cases if we are willing to exert a little effort to be present to others and allow others to be present to us—and, when our efforts seem to pass unrewarded, to remember not to catastrophize or overly personalize the unwanted results.

Good Projects and Activities

As well as reading and friendship, undertaking good activities and projects is also very spiritually fulfilling. But what we term as "good" activities might surprisingly not fit the bill.

A number of years ago a very close friend of mine in his early forties was dying from brain cancer. He was outrageous and we constantly teased one another. Even though he was dying, this did not stop.

He had been living in New York and I hadn't seen much of him since I was the best man at his wedding. When he was hospitalized in Philadelphia to undergo experimental treatment, I visited him. When I came to visit he had already been there for almost two weeks.

When I inquired about his health he shared a summary of his condition which included loss of short term memory. So, I said to him: "You mean you can't even remember what happened yesterday?" He said: "No."

"So," I said, "if I were here yesterday you wouldn't remember my visit?" He said: "No."

Then I smiled and said: "So, you don't remember me coming in and sitting here with you each day for five hours for the past two weeks?" He looked at me, hesitated for a second or two, grinned widely, and said...well, I can't share *exactly* what he said—after all this is a spiritual book—but we both had a good laugh together over it.

One of the things he did surprise me with, though, was a question which really helped me put my activities in perspective. He asked: "What good things are you doing now?" As I started to launch into an obsessive (naturally well-organized) list of my recent academic and professional accomplishments, he interrupted me by saying: "No, not that stuff. I mean what *really* good things have you done? When have you gone fishing last? What museums have you visited lately? What good movies have you seen in the past month?"

The "good things" he was speaking about the last time I saw him alive were different from the ones I in my arrogant good health thought about. Unfortunately, I have a lot of company in this regard. One rabbi once said that he never went to a home after the father of a family had died in which he heard the complaint: "He worked too *little.*" Too often our world whirls along, and the faster it goes, the less apt are nourishing activities to be included in our daily or weekly schedules. What a shame that the Lord gives us this world to enjoy and we just don't know what to do with it.

Joining a museum so we can visit it as we would an old friend, seeing new worlds geographically, dramatically, and psychologically through the lens of the director of a recently released movie, and going fishing or walking through the revitalized area of an old city were all on the list of my friend's "good things." They should be on ours as well.

When we join a local museum we can visit it at our leisure, stay as long as we like and look at as few or as many pieces as we wish. Rather than trying to conquer it we can make friends with the different pieces of art and learn its high points and deficiencies like the beautiful traits and wants of any good friend.

Movies also offer us a chance to broaden our horizons, fill our hearts, and challenge our spirits. The themes in movies often help us to look at the themes in our own lives. They help us wake up to the need for commitment, friendship, and courage.

But, as in the case of the books we read, we need to open up our options. So often I feel pressed by my own work with people and their difficulties that I think to myself: "The last thing I want to see is a movie with a message!" Maybe you feel the same at times. However, even when we are under pressure, sometimes seeing how others deal with theirs in creative, occasionally outrageous ways can offer us new life.

I remember going to dinner and a movie with my wife to celebrate her birthday. Since it was her birthday, she would get to choose the movie, and I suspected it would be one of those most dangerous of movies: "a socially-redeeming one." But I decided it was her birthday, so go I would. (I thought going might even save me some time in purgatory after I died—you see, old Catholic beliefs don't disappear, we just save them for the right moment!)

The movie she chose didn't even *sound* appealing. However, I went and, much against my earlier prejudices, found myself totally fascinated by it. Later I even told my graduate students that if they wanted a real slice of life and a good time to boot, they should go to see the movie "Fried Green Tomatoes."

Missing good experiences in life because of prejudgment on our part, or being unwilling to let good friends suggest new avenues for nourishment, is a real shame when it happens. But the good news is that there is something we can do about it now by opening ourselves up a bit more through expanding our tastes and interests.

Leisurely Walks/Stretching Our Legs

Taking a leisurely walk is also a beautiful way to fill our hearts. Whether it is a stroll through the country or just down a city block to go to the deli, a walk allows us to stretch our legs, get an oxygen exchange not possible in the buildings we populate which have recycled air, and see the slow changes in the weather, people, and environment around us.

Leisurely walks are not meant to accomplish something. Yet reward us they do. They allow us to gain a perspective not possible when locked up in our houses or offices. They even help us offer the grateful prayer to

God for our ability to walk, and they give us perspective by helping us remember we have a limited time only to walk and enjoy this earth.

I find that even stretching my legs by pacing a bit around the house is enjoyable; I stretch my mind as well as my legs in doing this. It is also a wonderful time to be grateful for all that I have been gifted with in life.

A number of years ago I was leading a retreat in the south of Thailand near the old Gulf of Siam. During one of the sessions before the heat of the day overtook us, I asked people to share what they thought prayer was. In response a former student of mine who happened to be posted in Thailand looked directly at me and said: "Well, it is many things. I really learned this to some extent from you."

"How?" I replied in a puzzled tone because I didn't even remember our discussing prayer.

"Well, when I was back in the United States," he said, "I called you at home to ask a question and I prefaced it with the statement: 'I hope I didn't disturb you.' To this you replied: 'Not at all. I was just practicing a new prayer form. It includes: pacing around the house, looking out each window while drinking a bit of coffee, smoking an awful-smelling cigar, and giving thanks to God that I have been so blessed. It's just great!'"

Walking, moving around in any form, is good. At the very least it helps us get out of ourselves enough so we can gain the perspective that is often lost when we get preoccupied. Walking is a sure antidote to unnecessary moodiness.

Good Yearnings...Good Nourishment

As was mentioned at the beginning, the above suggestions are not meant to be a comprehensive list at all but only some ideas on how to spur our thinking regarding "good food" for the soul. In addition to our whims and induced needs, the inner life has good yearnings. Good yearnings bring us to the edge of a new spiritual field filled with the riches of potentially rewarding relationships with old tattered books, new ideas, and an intricate tapestry of friends—some known, some unique, some challenging, all good.

We need to be open to what is right before us and enjoy new worlds of books, museums, relationships and experiences with nature. We need to start to let these forms of nourishment fill us with joy and perspective.

There is so much there for us if we look. As a matter of fact, once we start realizing what nourishment is actually available, rather than spiritual boredom, we will have to decide instead the answer to the question: What should I enjoy or experience *next?*

The Lord's comment to his disciples that to those who have been given much, more will be given is borne out when we get involved in activities and experiences that are truly renewing rather than mesmerizing.

In New Zealand, some nurseries plant kiwi fruit vines near other plants because the kiwi fruit attract bees. The bees then pollinate not only the kiwi but the other plants as well. The same can be said about nurturing activities in which we get involved. Such food for our soul not only feeds us now but also opens up new possibilities that we might not have even considered. The wonderful possibilities are endless.

And so, we mustn't be bashful. We need to take in what God has provided for us. And, with respect to the enlivening spiritual food God gives us in the form of nourishing activities, as a guideline we need only use the following sage advice of that beautiful Muppet Miss Piggy who wisely once said:

"Never eat more than you can lift."[29]

With this in mind, let me close this chapter on nurturing our inner life with a brief, simple reflection of mine. I include it to summarize what has been suggested in this chapter on the topic of *ways to nurture a hopeful heart.*

~ *Nurturing a Hopeful Heart* ~

Read a bit

Listen to a favorite song

Call a friend

Remember a kindness

Help the poor

Keep perspective

Smile broadly

Laugh loudly

Close doors gently

Do what you can

Live gratefully

Relax for a moment

Breathe deeply

Tease yourself often

Take a quiet walk...

Tell God a funny story

—*Robert J. Wicks*

Epilogue

Take my yoke upon your shoulders and learn from me, for I am gentle and humble of heart. Your soul will find rest, for my yoke is easy and my burden light.

—Matthew 11:29-30

This book has been about peace, hope, and love...*our* peace, hope, and love as well as that experienced by those persons with whom we come into contact, either personally or through reflection and prayer. It was created to be a reminder to us to prepare for, and be sensitive to, the fullness of that time in life when we have sufficient experience to discern and share the essentials of life—in other words, our "spiritual wisdom years." It also contained words of encouragement for us to appreciate the nobility of living with a spirit of prayer and recollection so what we share with others can come from a peaceful, hopeful, and loving heart rather than a worrisome grasping mind.

Given these simple, yet important, goals, I have composed the following prayer as a way to close both busy days and this little book on the interior life. Its content, form and spirit were inspired by a prayer of the Dinka, a predominantly Christian people who live along the Nile in the Southern Sudan.

When you recite it, my wish is that it will fill your heart now, and in the future, with a quiet, gentle spirit of hope and peace. May it also close each of your days with a deep sense of trust so you can rest in a God who *truly* loves you.

~ *Evening Prayer* ~

Now, as I watch the fading soft colors of dusk,
I pause, breathe deeply, and remember You.
My heart is tired, yet I am filled with hope.
My body aches, but my spirit is at home.

As I stretch and lie down for the evening,
Let my worrying cease,
my tired muscles relax,
my nose stop running,
my plans wait for morning...
my heart be at *peace*.

Yes, let me sleep in Your arms
Until a fresh clear morning awakens me,
So I can greet You with *love*...once again.
Amen.

—*Robert J. Wicks*

~ *Notes* ~

1. Abraham Joshua Heschel, *The Insecurity of Freedom,* New York: Farrar, Straus, and Giroux, 1951, p. 79.

2. Abraham Joshua Heschel, "On Prayer," *Conservative Judaism,* Vol XXV, no. 1, 1970.

3. J. P. Dubois Dumee, "Renewal of Prayer," *Lumen Vitae,* 38, 3, 1983, pp. 273–274. Emphasis added.

4. I am indebted to the extensive help my wife Michaele gave me on this section and the one on "self-knowledge."

5. Brother Lawrence of the Resurrection, *The Practice of the Presence of God,* translated by John J. Delaney, New York: Doubleday, 1977.

6. Maxim Gorky, *Gorky: My Childhood,* London: Penguin, 1966, p. 173.

7. Stories like this one appear in Anthony de Mello's *One Minute Nonsense,* Chicago: Loyola University Press, 1992.

8. Abraham Joshua Heschel, *God in Search of Man,* New York: Farrar, Straus, and Giroux, 1955, p. 36.

9. Lionel Blue, *Lionel Blue,* Springfield, Ill.: Templegate, 1987, p. 28.

10. Quotes like this one appear in the wonderful collection by Carolyn Warner, *The Last Word: A Treasury of Women's Quotes,* Englewood Cliffs, N.J.: Prentice Hall, 1992, p. 206.

11. See also: Francis Dorff's "Meditative Writing" in the *Handbook of Spirituality for Ministers,* edited by R. Wicks, Mahwah, N.J.: Paulist Press, 1995, pp. 153–173,

and Ronald Klug, *How to Keep a Spiritual Journal,* Minneapolis: Augsburg, 1982.

12. Statement by Albert Schweitzer cited in Gilbert Hay, *This Way to Happiness,* New York: Simon and Schuster, 1967, p. 35.

13. Robert J. Wicks, *Availability: The Problem and the Gift,* Mahwah, N.J.: Paulist Press, 1986, p. 42.

14. Ibid., p. 43.

15. A slightly different version of this story appeared in Warner's *The Last Word,* p. 147.

16. I am grateful to Eloise Wilding for sharing this story with me.

17. A version of this story appeared in Warner's *The Last Word,* p. 174. The author is unknown.

18. Anthony de Mello, *Awareness,* New York: Doubleday, 1990, pp. 104, 105.

19. Quoted in Warner's *The Last Word,* p. 48.

20. Donald McNeil, Douglas A. Morrison, and Henri J. M. Nouwen, *Compassion,* New York: Doubleday, 1982.

21. Heschel, *The Insecurity of Freedom,* p. 39. Emphasis added.

22. Quoted in Warner's *The Last Word,* p. 211.

23. Trevanian, *Summer of Katya,* New York: Crown, 1983, p. 44.

24. Daniel Easterman, *The Ninth Buddha,* New York: Doubleday, 1989, p. 530.

25. Matina S. Horner, "Introduction to The Radcliffe Biography Series," in *Dorothy Day* by Robert Coles, Reading, Mass: Addison-Wesley, 1987, p. ix.

26. Heschel, *God in Search of Man,* p. 168.

27. Quoted in Warner's *The Last Word,* p. 205.
28. Ibid., p. 138.
29. Ibid., p. 227.

~ *Readings* ~

The following simple books are helpful for nurturing the interior life. Even those which have been read before may well be worth reading again; for as we change and grow, so does what we gain from spiritual sources.

Bloom, Anthony, *Beginning to Pray*. Mahwah, NJ: Paulist Press, 1970.

Burrows, Ruth, *Guidelines for Mystical Prayer*. Denville, NJ: Dimension Books, 1980.

Conn, Joann Wolski, ed., *Women's Spirituality*. Mahwah, NJ: Paulist Press, 1986.

de Mello, Anthony, *Awareness*. New York: Doubleday, 1990.

———, *The Way to Love*. New York: Doubleday, 1992.

Donnelly, Doris, *Spiritual Fitness*. San Francisco: Harper, 1993.

Durka, Gloria, *Praying with Hildegard of Bingen*. Winona, MN: Saint Mary's Press, 1991.

———, *Praying with Julian of Norwich*. Winona, MN: Saint Mary's Press, 1989.

Fischer, Kathleen, *Autumn Gospel*. Mahwah, NJ: Paulist Press, 1995.

———, *Women at the Well*. Mahwah, NJ: Paulist Press, 1988.

Hall, Thelma, *Too Deep for Words*. Mahwah, NJ: Paulist Press, 1988.

Harrington, Wilfred, *The Tears of God*. Collegeville, MN: Liturgical Press, 1992.

Harris, Maria, *Dance of the Spirit.* New York: Bantam Books, 1989.

Leech, Kenneth, *True Prayer.* San Francisco: Harper, 1980.

McNeil, D., J. Morrison, and H. Nouwen, *Compassion.* New York: Doubleday, 1982.

Merton, Thomas, *New Seeds of Contemplation.* New York: New Directions, 1961.

——, *The Way of Chang Tzu.* New York: New Directions, 1961.

——, *The Wisdom of the Desert.* New York: New Directions, 1965.

Metz, Barbara, and John Burchill, *The Enneagram and Prayer.* Denville, NJ: Dimension Books, 1987.

Morneau, Robert, *Mantras from a Poet: Jessica Powers.* Kansas City, MO: Sheed and Ward, 1991.

Nouwen, Henri, *Making All Things New.* San Francisco: Harper, 1981.

——, *Reaching Out.* New York: Doubleday, 1975.

——, *The Way of the Heart.* New York: Seabury, 1981.

Rupp, Joyce, *Dear Heart, Come Home.* New York: Crossroad, 1996.

——, *Little Pieces of Light...Darkness and Personal Growth.* Mahwah, NJ: Paulist Press, 1994.

——, *May I Have This Dance?* Notre Dame, IN: Ave Maria Press, 1992.

Schmidt, Joseph, *Praying Our Experiences.* Winona, MN: St. Mary's Press, 1980.

Wiederkehr, Macrina, *Seasons of Your Heart.* San Francisco, Harper, 1991.

In addition to the above, you may also enjoy selections from two series. Paulist Press offers Spiritual Samplers, works of Christian heritage that include both classical and enduring twentieth-century writings that speak to the concerns of contemporary believers. Current and forthcoming titles include works by Julian of Norwich, Hildegard of Bingen, Francis and Clare, Meister Eckhart, and Teresa of Avila as well as selections of morning prayer, evening praise, and devotional poems. Ave Maria Press publishes 30 Days with a Great Spiritual Teacher, writings that make accessible the experience and wisdom of influential spiritual figures in history. Current and forthcoming titles deal with Augustine, Catherine of Siena, *The Cloud of Unknowing*, John of the Cross, Brother Lawrence, Thérèse of Lisieux, and Thomas à Kempis.